The **KIDS'** Guide

ANTI-RACISM

W

FRANKLIN WATTS

LONDON•SYDNEY

First published in Great Britain in 2022
by Hodder & Stoughton

Copyright © Hodder & Stoughton Limited, 2022

Editor: Victoria Brooker
Design: Thy Bui
Ilustrator: Scott Garrett

ISBN: 978 1 4451 8138 7 (hbk)
ISBN: 978 1 4451 8139 4 (pbk)

Printed in China

Franklin Watts
An imprint of Hachette Children's Group
Part of Hodder & Stoughton
Carmelite House
50 Victoria Embankment
London EC4Y 0DZ

An Hachette UK Company
www.hachette.co.uk
www.hachettechildrens.co.uk

The **KIDS'** Guide

# ANTI-RACISM

ARIKE OKE
& SCOTT GARRETT

# INTRODUCTION

You may be reading this book because you want to know more about what racism is and how to stop it happening.

Maybe you are being bullied and you think it could be racial bullying.

Perhaps you know someone who is being treated badly because of racism, and you want to help them.

Perhaps you are worried that you might be behaving in a racist way and you want to know how to stop.

You might even be curious about someone's cultural experiences but you are worried about how to ask them questions without offending them.

This book can help you spot racism and stop it in its tracks. If everyone bands together racism will become ... extinct!

# HOW WILL I SPOT RACISM?

**Racism is when someone thinks another person is less than them because of their:**

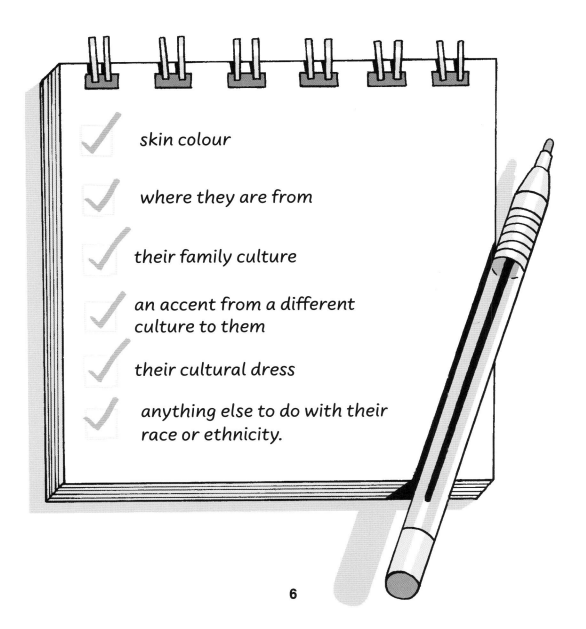

- skin colour
- where they are from
- their family culture
- an accent from a different culture to them
- their cultural dress
- anything else to do with their race or ethnicity.

Being treated unfairly because of racism is called RACIAL DISCRIMINATION.

If someone uses racist thinking as a reason to bully you with their actions or their words, this is racial bullying.

# WHAT DOES IT FEEL LIKE?

Racism and racial bullying can happen in lots of different ways. It always hurts, but it's not always obvious why, or how, it is hurting someone. That's the tricky thing about racism. It can be almost *invisible*.

**Racism and racial bullying can make you feel:**

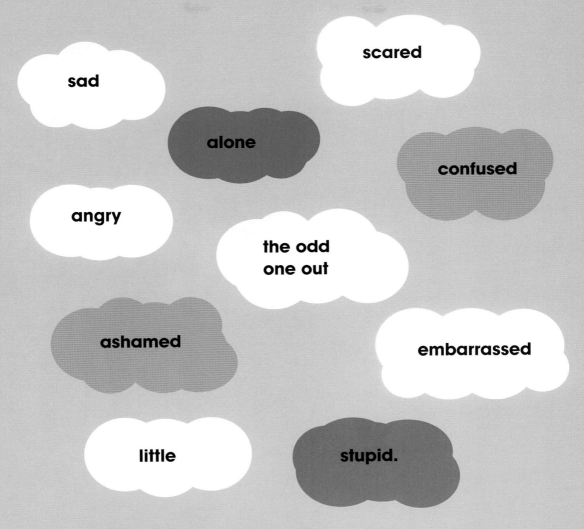

sad

scared

alone

confused

angry

the odd one out

ashamed

embarrassed

little

stupid.

Even if the racism isn't directed at you personally, you might still experience these feelings. You can be affected by racism experienced by your friends, or if you overhear someone being racist.

# WHAT HAPPENS?

There are lots of ways that racism can show itself, such as:

being beaten up

name calling

having your stuff stolen or damaged

seeing racist graffiti

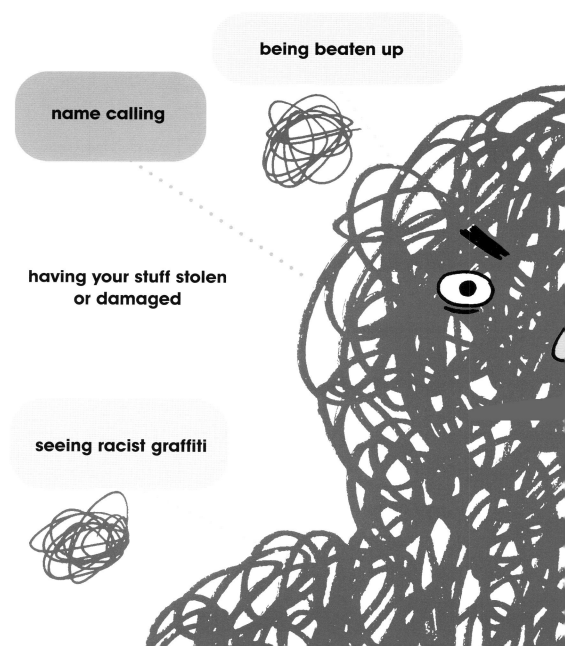

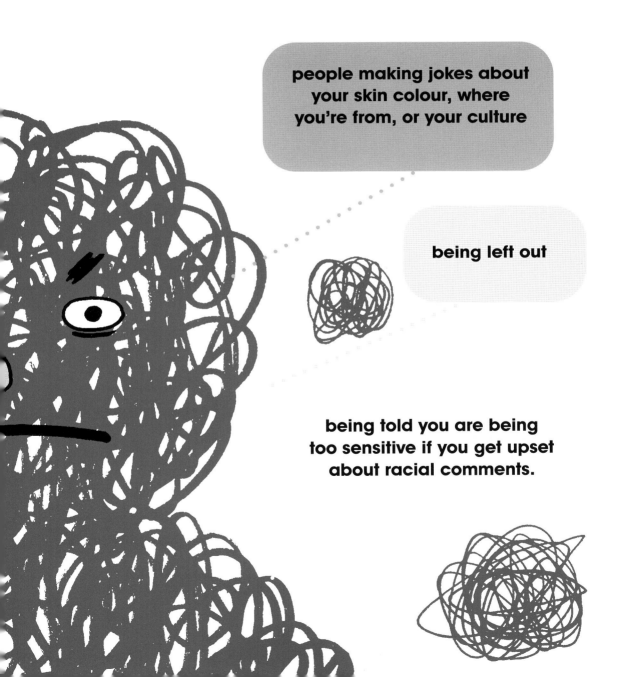

comments made about
how you dress or speak

people making jokes about
your skin colour, where
you're from, or your culture

being left out

being told you are being
too sensitive if you get upset
about racial comments.

# RACISM ISN'T FUNNY

Anyone can be racist. Because we are all brought up in our own particular cultures, it can be easy to think that anything different from our own family or local culture is wrong.

Sometimes people we love, such as our family and friends, can behave in a racist way, such as making jokes about someone else's culture. They might not know, understand or care, how much even a joke can hurt other people.

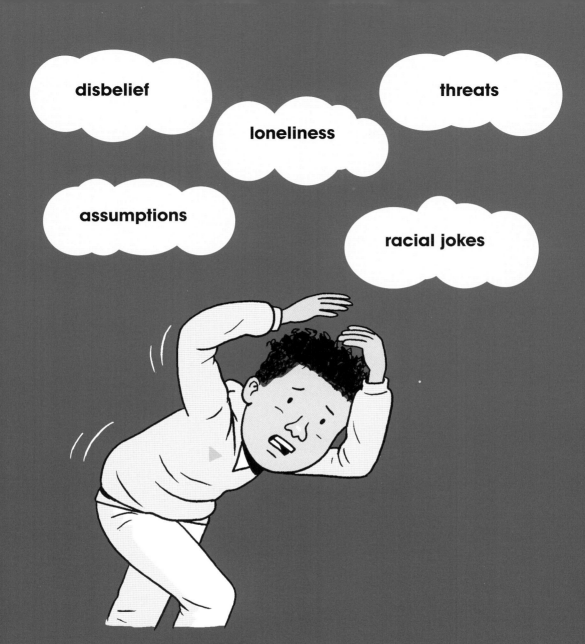

Even comments that seem small, or like a joke, can build up to make you feel as if you have to change who you are, and that you don't fit in.

# SEARCHING FOR SAFETY

**Sometimes, world events can make racism grow.**

**Climate change and war can make people have to move far from their homes around the world to a new, safer, place to live.**

People in this situation are refugees and asylum seekers. They aren't always given a kind welcome when they arrive in their new country, when racism has made people in their new communities suspicious of them.

Racism can make a sad and scary situation, such as moving across the planet to find safety, worse.

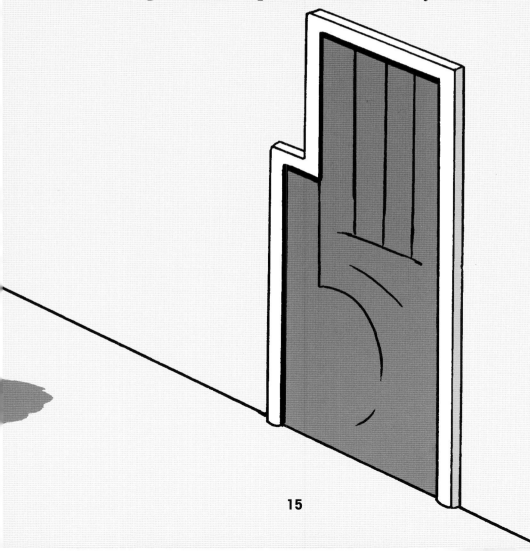

# PEOPLE DON'T FIT IN BOXES!

One of the greatest things about humans is that
we can see patterns. Seeing patterns helps us work
out maths problems. It helps us design buildings,
write songs and figure out the laws of science.
But sometimes being able to see patterns leads
us to create assumptions and stereotypes.

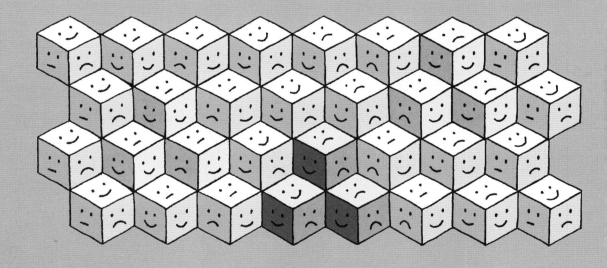

A stereotype is a fixed idea about a person or
a thing. It's a stereotype that princesses live in
castles. But princesses don't always live in castles.

It's a stereotype that all scientists wear white coats and glasses, or all librarians wear cardigans.

Stereotypes are sticky. It's hard to remove them.

Harmful stereotypes about people include ones about their skin colour and cultures. Harmful stereotypes sort people into boxes of 'types of person', instead of the truth that we are all unique!

# SPEAK UP, SPEAK OUT

You might think,

'I'm not racist.
This isn't my problem.'

Imagine being a farmer. Your neighbour's field is on fire. Your field's not on fire, so you don't help. But the fire spreads to the other neighbouring farms.

Even though the fire doesn't reach your field, all of your neighbours lose their farms. If you'd helped to put out the first fire, everyone's farms could have been saved.

Not being racist is like seeing a fire but not helping to put it out. Being anti-racist means helping to put out the fire. It means being active against racism. This book gives some tips about how to be anti-racist in a positive and safe way.

Being anti-racist is like a superpower that stops stereotypes sticking, and it's something that everyone can be.

# RACISM CAN SPREAD

Sometimes racism can appear in a flash like a bolt of lightning!

If you only know one person who has a difference to you, and they treat you badly, you might start to assume that everyone with that difference is a bad person too. This isn't fair, but it can be hard to move on from this kind of assumption. It helps to watch out for assumptions that you or your friends might be making.

**Do the ANTI-RACISM WORKOUT!**

Ask yourself where your ideas
about other people come from.

Jump at the chance
to be kind instead
of cruel.

Challenge yourself
to find out facts instead
of making assumptions.

# CLUB CULTURE

Have you ever joined a club? Being in a club can be cool. You can get special treats for being part of a club. Maybe it's a football club and you get your club kit and can use the club's pitch. Maybe it's an after-school club and you get to do activities with other people in the club. These special treats for members are called privileges.

Depending on your skin colour and racial culture you might automatically get privileges that other people will never have access to, including not being discriminated against. It's like being in a club that you can't choose to join or leave.

Looking out for when you are treated better than others, and then making sure to help out people who don't have your privileges, is part of being ANTI-RACIST.

# BOYE'S STORY

Boye moved to a new area with his parents. He was excited to go to a new school and make new friends. On his first day he looked around. No one else looked like him.

At break he wanted to join in a game of football. The other boys let him join in, but when he missed a goal they started to tease him. They said that he should be good at football because of how he looked. Boye felt embarrassed.

In class, the teacher asked him to read out loud from a book. The class started laughing. Afterwards, a girl in his class told him that the children were surprised that people from Boye's country could read.

When he got home, Boye felt sad and lonely. He had never felt different and left out before.

# TRYING TO FIT IN

At school the next day, Boye tried to fit in. He changed the way he spoke, using the sort of words that the other kids used. When the other children made fun of him, he laughed along with them.

But inside he felt even more sad. He thought he would never be able to fit in, and he thought that it was his fault.

Boye's class teacher noticed that he was becoming more and more quiet. The teacher took Boye aside to talk about how he was feeling.

# HEROES WHO HELP

The next day, the teacher organised a special class project for everyone. They had to find out heroes from as many different cultures as they could. All of the children found out amazing facts, and Boye was surprised that he discovered lots of heroes who looked like him.

The teacher asked each table to discuss heroes from different cultures. Boye was nervous about what the children on his table would say. A few of his classmates asked Boye questions, but the questions were friendly. Boye started to feel a little more comfortable.

The next time that one of his classmates said something silly about Boye, a new friend stuck up for him. If Boye felt sad, he thought about the heroes class project which helped him feel happier again.

# STORIES ARE POWERFUL

Have you ever heard a ghost story that made you frightened of the dark? Have you ever watched a scary film that made you frightened of what might be under the bed?

Racism and racial stereotypes are like scary stories told so often over so many years to so many people that you start to think they might be true. Even people who are victims of racism might start to believe the stereotypes about themselves. That's how powerful stories are!

In reality, there are lots of stories we can share about each other. Cool stories about cooperation and adventure, sad stories about terrible things in the past, beautiful stories about culture and creativity.

Sharing real stories about the culture that we share and stories about what makes us different from each other changes the same old story and banishes stereotypes.

# SILENCE ISN'T THE ANSWER

Racism and other types of discrimination are against the law. It's important to report it.

A hate crime is a crime that involves prejudice and discrimination. It includes someone damaging your belongings or physically hurting you with racial bullying.

WHO TO TELL:

**At school:** A trusted teacher
**Outside of school:** An adult that you trust
**The police.** In an emergency you can call 999; at other times call 101.

You might need to tell more than one person.

Keep notes of what has happened – screenshots, photos, a diary – as evidence. This will help you describe what's happened.

It's discouraging if the first person you tell doesn't help. Try telling another person. Don't stop speaking up until someone listens.

# RECIPE FOR CONFIDENCE

You might feel worthless if you've experienced racism, or if you see racism and didn't act.

Try out this recipe to build up your self-worth. Gradually, you'll feel ready to be a champion for yourself and others.

## RECIPE

**STEP 1:**
Take 3 pinches of holding your head up high. How you hold your body can change how you feel inside.

**STEP 2:**
Mix with a generous dash of your favourite music that makes you feel positive about life.

**STEP 3:**

Add a dollop of being kind. Helping someone else, even if it's something small, such as asking if they're okay, can make you feel good too.

**STEP 4:**

Stir up your thoughts. You don't have to immediately respond to someone. Taking time to think about what to say can help you form a confident reply.

**STEP 5:**

Break the mould. Trying something new, such as joining a club, or a little thing, such as updating your online avatar, can give you a boost. You don't need to change who you are to try out new things.

# CURIOSITY QUIZZING

**You want to find out more about your friends' cultures, but how do you ask without being rude?**

**Here are a few tips to help:**

 Check the person is comfortable with being asked questions about their culture.

 Don't ask them to perform for you, for example, by asking them to speak in another language for no reason.

 Swap information. Maybe you could find out the meaning of your name, and see if your friend will share the meaning of their name.

Don't ask a question that's really a judgement, for example 'People where you're from don't go to school, do they?'

 Cultural holidays, such as Passover, Ramadan or Easter, are great times to be curious. Ask:

**How do your family celebrate?**

 Don't correct the person when they answer you. Trust that the person knows more about their own experience than you do.

# WHAT IF YOU EXPERIENCE OR SEE RACISM IN ACTION?

Stay safe! If someone has called you a racist name, or racially bullied you or your friends, don't try to get back at them. Keep your cool.

**Walk away.**

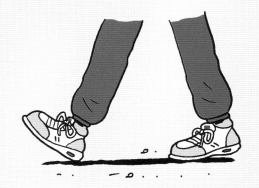

**Keep a record of what happened.**

**Tell an adult that you trust. This could be a parent, a teacher or a youth worker.**

**If they can't help, tell another adult that you trust.**

**Contact Childline for advice and help (see page 47).**

Sometimes you might experience or see racism in action in a situation where you feel safe to call it out. A friend of yours might make a racist joke. If you feel safe you could ...

**... tell them the joke isn't funny,**

**... show them this book,**

**... help anyone affected by the joke feel part of the group again by making it easy for them to join back in with the conversation or game.**

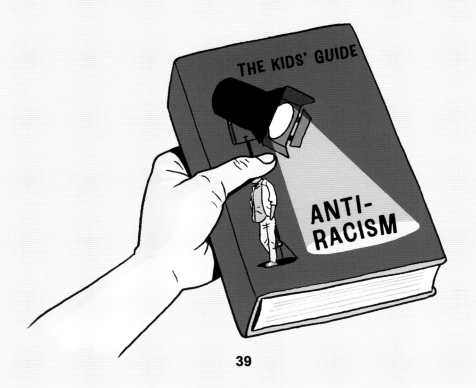

# LET'S STICK TOGETHER

Andi saw Sarita being picked on by bullies on her way home from school. Andi crossed the road to walk with Sarita. Sarita wasn't on her own anymore. The bullies backed off.

Roisin was crying at a table on her own in the canteen. Some bullies had written racist abuse on her bag. Mo and Jay took pictures of the damage and showed them to their class teacher, backing Roisin up when she reported what had happened.

Shobna shared her Diwali celebration sweets with her friends Dai and Rohan. Rohan invited Dai and Shobna to have traditional jollof rice with their family. Dai invited the friends to his confirmation at his church. The friends support each other through good times and bad times.

# DIGITAL DRAMA

Racism sneaks up on you online. Racial bullying seems invisible when it happens in an online forum, game, your phone or device. Here are some ways to protect yourself from racial bullying trolls.

**PRIVACY SETTINGS:** You can set up your accounts so only your friends and family can follow you online and send you messages.

**MUTE MAGIC:** Most online platforms will let you mute other users without telling them that you've muted them. Now you don't have to see unpleasant people's unpleasant messages and posts.

**BLOCK THE TROLL:** Blocking is one step on from using mute. Now the people causing you trouble online have no way of reaching you online.

**REPORT:** When you see something bad, report it. Racial bullying and racism is not allowed on social media platforms. The person you report will not know it was you. The social media platform will independently investigate the report.

**KEEP A RECORD:** Although it might be tricky, you should try to keep a record of what you've seen or been sent as evidence of the racist behaviour. This can help when you're ready to tell trusted adults about the abuse.

# THE END OF RACISM!

It can feel impossible to fight an invisible enemy like racism. Racism has been around for a long time and it lives off silence and ignorance.

**Keep talking about anti-racism.**

**Keep reporting racism.**

**Support each other.**

**Find out about other people's lives.**

**Stay safe – help is out there.**

**Find ways to be kind.**

**Give help.**

**Ask for help.**

**Question assumptions.**

**BELIEVE IN YOURSELF!**

Use this book and the sources of help on the next pages to help yourself and help others. Together, we can defeat racism for good!

# FURTHER INFORMATION

**Helplines** – You can use a helpline if you want to talk to someone about how you're feeling. Trained staff and volunteers will listen to you, and offer advice.

In the UK, you can call Childline for free on 0800 1111. They also have a website, childine.org.uk, which has useful pages about racism.

The Muslim Youth Helpline offers faith and culturally sensitive support by phone, live chat or email. You can email them at info@myh.org.uk or phone them on 0808 808 2008.

**Counsellors** – If you don't feel comfortable talking to people you know about your feelings, you could try and see a counsellor. Speaking in private to someone can be very useful.

# USEFUL WEBSITES

**Childline**
www.childline.org.uk/info-advice/bullying-abuse-safety/crime-law/racism-racial-bullying/
Find out more about racism. Watch some videos to find out about racial stereotypes and learn signs of racism.

**Young Minds**
www.youngminds.org.uk/young-person/coping-with-life/racism-and-mental-health/
Being treated differently or unfairly because of race, skin colour or ethnicity can negatively affect mental health. Find out more about how to improve your mental health and know how to report hate crime.

# BOOKS

*Black History Matters* by Robin Walker
(Franklin Watts, 2020)

*Dealing with Racism* by Jane Lacey
(Franklin Watts, 2019)

*I'm a Global Citizen: Culture and Diversity*
by Georgia Amson-Bradshaw (Franklin Watts, 2020)

*The History of the African and Caribbean Communities in Britain* by Hakim Adi (Wayland,2020)

# INDEX